The Art of Allowance

A Short, Practical Guide to Raising
Money-Smart, Money-Empowered Kids

The Art of Allowance

A Short, Practical Guide to Raising
Money-Smart, Money-Empowered Kids

John Lanza

For information about permission to reproduce selections from this book, write to info@snigglezoo.com or to Permissions, Snigglezoo Books, 419 N. Larchmont Blvd. #5, Los Angeles, CA 90004.

www.theartofallowance.com

Library of Congress Cataloging-in-Publication Data is available

ISBN 978-0-9826820-4-3

Book design by Todd Slater

Printed in the USA

3rd printing, 2018

"Any man who does not think that what he has
is more than ample, is an unhappy man,
even if he is the master of the whole world."

— Seneca (Greek Stoic)[1]

For Robert Day Thomas, My Granddad

With Granddad in 1978

Contents

Introduction

Black Beauty

My grandfather carefully inspected "Black Beauty," his first "horsey" bank. The bank was small and sleek with a two-inch hole in the top to receive coins.

"When did you start saving in it?" I asked.

"I can't remember not saving."

Growing up amidst Depression-Era breadlines and financial uncertainty had its silver lining.

Michael Pollan, author of *The Omnivore's Dilemma*, has a simple guideline when it comes to eating: "Don't eat anything your great-great-great grandmother wouldn't recognize as food."[2] Similarly, my grandfather's advice when I graduated college and headed off into the world was simple: "Understand compound interest, and live beneath your means."

My grandfather was probably the most money-smart, money-empowered person I'd ever met. He lived the advice he gave me. We can all learn from him.

"Black Beauty"

A Simple Mission

"My view of human nature is that all of us are only just holding it together in various ways,...and we just need to go easy with one another, knowing that we're all these incredibly fragile beings."

—Alain de Botton

If you're a parent like me, then you can probably relate to Alain de Botton's quote. Just trying to keep it together. Last night after dinner, my wife and I high-fived each other for our *remarkable* achievement...we fed our kids! This gesture simply underscores the difficulty of a pretty simple mission—to raise good kids.

If you've ever thought about why raising a child to be money-smart is so hard today, then you're in good company. There are strong forces working against it: omnipresent marketing, societal reluctance to discuss money openly and a feeling that there's just not enough time. Concurrently, with the fraying social safety net, disappearing pensions and the growing gig economy, we all must bear greater responsibility for our own financial well-being. Our children's responsibility will inevitably increase. Our kids will *need* financial smarts to thrive.

In reading this book, you've made an important decision to begin teaching your child money smarts. I don't take your choice lightly, and I'm here to help. When you consider the societal stressors associated with money troubles—indebtedness, relationship strain and less freedom, to name a few—what could be more important than choosing to teach your child money smarts? Being in control of money does not ensure happiness, but a lack of monetary control often leads to misery.

I wrote this book to help you raise a money-smart, money-empowered child. You will create an allowance program to help your child learn the real-world, core money-smart skills: *distinguishing needs from wants, making smart money choices* and *saving for goals.* You and your child will develop your own *Art of Allowance* as she takes control of her money and learns to use it as a tool. I use "she" or "he" interchangeably throughout this book, as *The Art of Allowance* applies to both your daughters and your sons.

Becoming money-empowered will be a journey for your child. First, she will learn money smarts, the building blocks for a money-empowered foundation. A money-empowered person knows money is a tool and uses it to craft a meaningful life. A money-empowered person thinks through purchases and spends intelligently on items of value and meaning. She gives to charity—or, in the parlance of this book, she "shares" her money with those less fortunate than herself—at the level she finds fulfilling. She also saves for bigger-ticket items. This plan of action includes her having enough money to enjoy all of life's phases, from young adulthood through retirement. She puts needs first and compartmentalizes her indulgences in keeping with her beliefs.

Nobody's Perfect

Before we take these first steps, please know that I am not a paragon of perfection when it comes to teaching our own kids to be money-smart. Sure, my wife and I got them started early. From a young age, our children learned to employ the goal-setting and visualization techniques I'll discuss later. Like any parent, however, I get lazy from time to time. You will too, and that's okay.

Raising a money-smart child is a bit like meditation. You're not looking for a 100% clear mind. That's impossible. You're building mindfulness in bits and pieces. You may be distracted at first before you settle in and find more mental stillness as time goes on.

Starting a dialogue about money with your child is a huge step forward in the journey you will take together. Be kind to yourself if you 1) miss a week of allowance payment, 2) let him lose track of a savings goal or 3) allow him to forget completely about one of the jars I'll help you set up. We'll discuss how to avoid these issues, but life happens. When you hit a bump in the road, always try to keep the big picture in mind—your intention to raise a money-smart, money-empowered child.

We'll get into bigger issues like protecting ourselves and our families from the invasion of *stuff*. Many parents have asked me how they can raise less materialistic kids. This book is in part an attempt to help you do that. *Stuff* is at the core of materialism, and this book addresses this issue head-on. Similarly, we'll discuss how money should not be used as a metric to determine societal value.

Although we may want to believe that giving a periodic sum of money called "allowance" is the magic dust to help grow a money-smart, money-empowered child, the truth is that there is no magic dust. In fact, starting an allowance is where this process gets real. You will replace abstractions like "saving for a rainy day" with saving for actual goals.

Armed with money, your child will begin to make tangible choices. She'll make mistakes, and the small error now will help her avoid the big blunder later. You'll want to give her some autonomy, and now is the time for you to step up as her guide rather than to step back entirely. Passivity is where many allowance programs go awry. You are her active guide. This book is your manual.

While I can help you on this journey, this book is called *The Art of Allowance* because you will apply your own parenting skills and understanding of your unique child to craft your own program based on the guidelines presented in this book. You'll get the tools you need to help your child along the path to becoming money-smart and money-empowered.

You're making an important choice—that you will be the one to teach your child about money. You're also making an investment of time—your most valuable asset—to motivate her to move towards this goal. I want to help you get there.

Our Story

Our own journey began innocently enough. My wife and I were driving with our then six-month-old daughter to Big Bear, an idyllic little getaway just outside of our Southern California home. Naturally, we talked about our family plans, and the discussion soon turned to how we might raise a money-smart child.

My wife had always been money-smart. She saved for and bought her dream car, a Jeep Wrangler, in her early twenties. Paid for in cash. No debt. As you'll read shortly, I took a little longer to figure things out. We wondered how this disparity happened. Both of us came from frugal families. My dad was even a banker!

We set a goal to actively raise money-smart, money-empowered kids. We didn't want to leave the results to chance, and our goal inspired us to conceive *The Money Mammals* program. I knew that we needed to engage kids—to get them excited—to become money-smart. Not an easy task.

As we developed materials and programs to support this initial mission, I began to realize fully the importance of parental involvement in the process. After creating a DVD, three picture books, mobile apps and more materials designed to engage kids, it was time for me to write my first book for you, the parents.

Why This Book Is for You

As a fellow parent whose time is in demand, I tried to make this book a quick, easy read. Sure, learning *The Art of Allowance* takes time, but doing so should not be a *major* time burden.

Although I believe this book is appropriate for folks of all means, I know that our family is incredibly fortunate not to want for the basics. Yet, the importance of raising a money-smart child is independent of economic class. Families rich, poor and in-between can benefit from this book with gratitude for what they have.

With fair warning, the ideas presented in this book may challenge you as they have many families, including mine. You may have developed some unhealthy money habits over the years that you want to change. For example, I became much more aware that the rush of an "exciting" purchase was fleeting when I observed that feeling repeated in our own children. Engage your curiosity, and be kind to yourself. Reflect upon, but don't dwell on, the past. I've found my own personal change in this process to be rewarding. If you're open to change, I believe you will be rewarded too.

Wanting your kids to do right where you went wrong is normal. At times, I felt ill-equipped to teach our kids money smarts, especially about investing, which I discuss. That notion hasn't prevented me from talking with them about investing basics and those core money-smart skills to provide them a solid foundation to become money-empowered and perhaps better investors than their parents.

The Art of Allowance is a team game. Engage your child-rearing partner if you're fortunate enough to have one. This action may lead to some difficult discussions. *Have those discussions.* Work to resolve whatever money disagreements you may have. You don't have to agree about everything, but a united front makes this process much easier. The *more* of your family you involve, the better (and easier): mother, brother, grandparent, sister and even mother-in-law!

Still, you may be wondering if this book is for *you*. I have yet to meet someone—seriously, *anyone*—who doesn't think teaching his own kids to be money-smart from an early age is a great idea. I wrote this book to fill the void between agreeing with and executing on this idea. I'm confident there will be at least *something* in this book you'll find useful. If not, contact me, and I'll give your money back.

How This Book Works

I've attempted to synthesize my direct experiences with our kids, other families and current research on parenting, children, money and motivation. I discovered that there are many opinions about allowance (Just ask the next person you meet!), and most of them are uninformed and based on whatever we may or may not have learned from our parents.

This book will continue to emphasize the core skills I mentioned early on: *saving for goals, distinguishing needs from wants* and *making smart money choices.* I'll walk you through setting up an allowance with your child. You'll learn about the weekly distribution into the three jars—*Share, Save* and *Spend Smart*—and tactics to deal with bumps along the way.

Your maturing child will be ready for more money responsibility as she grows. I'll outline how you can "upgrade" her allowance to move her along the money-empowered path. I'll touch upon opening up bank accounts, offer you some thoughts on investing and discuss how early money failures may help your child avoid larger financial catastrophes down the road.

Along the way, you will develop your own allowance program that works for your specific child. This book is less about telling and more about guiding you. By working with your particular parenting style, you'll learn to master *The Art of Allowance* and to raise your own money-smart, money-empowered child.

Throughout the book, I will address "bigger picture" topics to provide a broader context for the journey you and your child are beginning. As some of these sections may feel like tangents (sadly, it's hereditary), you can consume this book the way my little brother used to prioritize his dinner plate. Meat and carbs first. Veggies? Only if you're in the mood!

Start with the meat—the allowance lessons—if you like, or eat a more balanced meal as you go. Either way, I think you'll be satisfied with the fare. I've marked these special "veggie" sections as "Memos from the Chief Mammal." While I think they make for a tasty narrative when read as presented, feel free to leave them on your plate if you wish.

Why am I the Chief Mammal? As I mentioned before, I created *The Money Mammals* program. I never liked the term CEO. Too corporate. I remembered that Maxine Clark, CEO of Build-A-Bear Workshop, called herself the Chief Executive Bear. Until I had my own business, I thought the concept a little corny. However, I realized that I never forgot her title, *and* it always made me smile. That's why I'm the Chief Mammal.

Ready for your first serving of veggies?

---

[1] This statement has been attributed to both Seneca and Epicurus. For more information, please reference Seneca's "Letter 9: On Philosophy and Friendship" in *Letters from a Stoic: Epistulae Morales ad Lucilium*.
[2] Pollan, Michael. "Six Rules for Eating Wisely." *MichaelPollan.com*, June 4, 2006, www.michaelpollan.com/articles-archive/six-rules-for-eating-wisely.

Memo from the Chief Mammal:
Beware of *Stuff*

*"We amass material things for the same reason
that we eat—to satisfy a craving."*
—Marie Kondo

Stuff. It's the elephant in the room. In some cases,
this metaphor is almost literal.

Psychologists Edward Deci and Richard Ryan noted
in their self-determination theory that three human
needs are required to live a fulfilled life: autonomy,
competence and relatedness.[3] If we are in pursuit
of or have lives filled with appropriate amounts of
each, then we are much more likely to be happy,
fulfilled or, as Krista Tippett of *On Being* prefers to
say, "flourishing."[4]

Autonomy is essentially freedom. (We drive the car.)
Competence refers to our ability to be experts at
something. (We fix the car.) Relatedness is genuine
human interaction. (We drive our fixed car to a
friend's house to sing karaoke, bake cookies and
play Settlers of Catan.)

Did you notice what is missing from Deci and Ryan's
imperatives? *Stuff!* How many of us recognize the
inability of *stuff* to provide fulfillment as we find
ourselves at the mall with shopping bags in hand?
I'm from New Jersey. We know malls. We know
stuff. If a boy from Jersey can learn that *stuff* is not

fulfilling, then anyone can.

Stuff can provide only momentary jolts of excitement—not happiness in the larger sense. Understanding the power that *stuff* holds over us is critical as we begin the process of raising money-smart, money-empowered kids.

We don't need to feel guilty for wanting. We do, however, need to know exactly *why* we want. Is it a desire planted by marketers? Or is it something that saves us time, our most precious resource? Are we engaging in "retail therapy" to heal emotional wounds?[5] If we're fulfilling an emotional void with *stuff,* then we probably want it for the wrong reasons. The rush we receive from *stuff* is *always* fleeting.

A restaurant that makes our taste buds sing may be a fulfilling *experience.* My wife and I enjoy going out to dinner. We love food. Plus, it gives us a much-needed respite from the kids. (And if you go on half-price Monday, then hooray for you!) Experiences matter.

My dad keeps a lot of memorabilia he's collected through the years and gets a lot of enjoyment sharing it with old friends. In a sense, he's creating new experiences, and I wouldn't typically classify these mementos as *stuff.* In the words of Marie Kondo, author of *The Life-Changing Magic of Tidying Up,* these items "spark joy" for him.[6]

Thinking about what experiences and items are meaningful to you is worthwhile. Understanding what drives us makes it easier to help our kids learn to avoid the scourge of *stuff* perhaps earlier than we did.

[3] Ryan, Richard M. and Edward L. Deci. "Self-Determination Theory and the Facilitation of Intrinsic Motivation, Social Development, and Well-Being." *American Psychologist* 55.1 (2000): 68. See also: Pink, Daniel. *Drive: The Surprising Truth About What Motivates Us* (New York: Penguin Group, 2011), 71-73.
[4] "Calming Philosophies for Chaotic Times—Krista Tippett." *The Tim Ferriss Show with Tim Ferriss. The Tim Ferriss Blog*, February 21, 2017, https://tim.blog/2017/02/21/krista-tippett/.
[5] Plastow, Michael. "Retail Therapy: The Enjoyment of the Consumer." *British Journal of Psychotherapy* 28.2 (2012): 206-07.
[6] Kondo, Marie. *The Life-Changing Magic of Tidying Up: The Japanese Art of Decluttering and Organizing.* Berkeley: Ten Speed Press, 2014.

1
—

Getting Started

The Three Jars

"The scariest moment is always just before you start."

—*Stephen King*

When my wife and I created *The Money Mammals* over a decade ago, we helped introduce a generation of kids to three jars: *Share, Save* and *Spend Smart.* Though the three-jar paradigm already existed, we added *"Smart"* to the *Spend* jar. I felt that visually reminding kids to use their noggins when making spending decisions was important. ("Smart" also sounded a lot better in *The Money Mammals* theme song.)

Punt the Pig

The piggy bank has been asking to be put out to pasture since its birth. What a crappy receptacle for cash! Have you ever tried to extract paper money from one? It's excruciating. Some piggy banks are even designed to be *destroyed* in order to access the money. How does that make any sense? Hey, piggy, it's *my* money! Don't make me use this hammer. So wasteful. So inhumane!

We're aiming for transparency. That's why I recommend you punt the pig and use three *clear* jars.

At this point, you might be thinking...

"We're going to let him see his money accumulate?"

"Heaven forbid!"

"We're going to let our five-year-old put his money in the collection plate?"

"What if he eats it before it makes it up the aisle?"

*"We're going to let him take the money **out** of the Spend Smart jar to **spend** it...maybe even on **trivial** stuff?"*

"That's IT! I'm calling the authorities!"

Remember, we are ultimately trying to raise a money-empowered child. Empowerment is our watchword. We're in it for the long haul, and we don't want to *hide* the money from him. We want to teach him how to be smart about the choices he has to make with his money. Money is neither good nor evil. Money is a neutral tool he can learn to wield like an artist's brush. You will teach him the skills to use it properly. Discuss it openly. Let him see and access his money easily.

Setting Up an Allowance

Okay, your jars are set up. You and your daughter have labeled them *Share, Save* and *Spend Smart*. Now what?

We all worry that she may run amok, spending money like a Kardashian. Don't let your worries turn into what I call "Spendthrift Syndrome," where you dole out a pittance because you don't trust her with money. Remember that the consequence of an empty jar may be a more powerful lesson than anything you say to her. The dilemma here is that in order to establish trust, you have to trust her with a meaningful allowance. Recognize *Spendthrift Syndrome* before it's too late, or you may hear something like this: "Yeah, Dad, thanks for my 75-cent allowance. I'll be able to get that Razor scooter I want in a few decades. Awesome."

This statement is not that far from reality. I know parents of means who were giving their seven-year-old 75 cents. He'll need seven months to save for the next volume of *Captain Underpants!* Remember, the purpose of an allowance is to teach your child to be responsible with his money. Be careful not to *under*-empower him.

The Art of Allowance means you have leeway to construct your own system—to distribute an amount that works for your family. It also means that you need to empower him fully with meaningful amounts. Otherwise, your program will be in jeopardy of failing before it starts.

Virtually every youth money expert agrees that a good starting point for an allowance is one dollar per the child's age per week. So, a five-year-old would receive five bucks per week. Pretty simple—nine bucks per week for your nine-year-old.

Of course, if your financial situation doesn't allow you

to use this guideline, then adjusting your allowance rate is sensible. Just don't err on the side of doing nothing.

How to "Nudge"

An easy foundational principle to teach your kids is how to make *choices*. Unfortunately, we—adults and children—aren't always so good at making the best choices for ourselves. Richard Thaler and Cass Sunstein point out this realization in *Nudge: Improving Decisions About Health, Wealth and Happiness*. They note, for example, that when an organization decides to "opt-in" people to a retirement savings program, employees are much more likely to invest in their retirement.[7] This action is something that most of us would agree is a good thing to do.

Similarly, we want to help our child "opt-in" to behaviors we are fairly certain will be good for him as he gets older. These behaviors may vary slightly from family to family—the *art* part of the allowance process. You will come up with your list of "opt-in" behavior choices to nudge your child forward.

For example, if your child receives a birthday check from Grandma, then he can choose to blow the money on a few packs of Pokémon cards, or you can nudge him with a guideline—half the check goes to saving for the bike he wants (or whatever goal is currently on his *Save* jar). Nudging can help him learn to make smarter choices.

Weekly Distribution

Weekly allowance distribution provides children with opportunities to make frequent choices. You can nudge them towards making smart decisions. Let's use the five-year-old's five-dollar allowance as an example. We would begin with an "opt-in" nudge, requiring her to put one dollar in her *Share* jar and one in her *Save* jar.

Save jar deposits help her begin to understand the idea that one should "pay oneself first," a maxim of virtually all good money experts. *Share* jar deposits are like little gratitude lessons. Don't be afraid to be literal about these lessons at first. Tell your daughter that she is "paying herself first" or "setting aside money for others."

The autonomy, where she is free to make her own choices, lies in the allowance balance—those three discretionary dollars that she can put anywhere. Shove them into the *Spend Smart* jar? Kids typically do. Drop another dollar into the *Share* jar? That's allowed too. Or perhaps she's saving for a goal and wants to direct more of her money into her *Save* jar. Advise her, but give her control of these dollars. For example, as we delve into goals and visualization in a bit, you can suggest that she can get that playset for which she's saving *faster* if she puts more money in the *Save* jar at allowance-distribution time. You can even use what I'll describe as *enhanced interest* or *incentivizing* to influence her choices.

We established transfer guidelines for our daughters. They could transfer money from their *Spend Smart* jars to their *Save* jars for a previously determined goal. *Save* jar money was not transferable. *Share* jar money had to go to a charitable cause. Thus, money could flow from the *Spend Smart* jar to any other jar but *not* vice versa. David McCurrach originally introduced me to transfer guidelines, and he defines more ground rules in his workbook *Allowance Magic: Turn Your Kids into Money Wizards.*[8] (This tool and many other resources can be found at *theartofallowance.com.*)

Although I recommend starting an allowance at age five, all is not lost if you begin with your eight-year-old. Even your tween (a 10- to 12-year-old) or teenager has much to gain. Of course, starting early is important because of the seemingly inverse relationship between your child's age and her perception of your own intelligence.

What Kind of Gazelle Is Your Child?

You've likely heard the joke about the two young gazelles. They see a lion in the grass getting ready to pounce. One gazelle looks at the other and says, "Are you faster than a lion?" The other gazelle glances back and remarks, "I don't have to be faster than a lion. I just have to be faster than you."

Observe your child. Is he like the fast or slow gazelle? Both creatures are trying to outrun the lion—here a beast of financial illiteracy, consumption, *stuff* and other temptations which make it formidable.

If you have a fast gazelle, then pat yourself on the back. He may be suited to financial literacy lessons from the get-go. If he takes to goal saving quickly, then you can accelerate his training. He might be that child who is always thinking about how to use his money more effectively. The beast will never catch him. Lucky you!

If you have a slow gazelle, then give yourself *several* pats on the back. He really needs the help you can provide. Starting the money dialogue early can help him become money-smart and eventually money-empowered, enabling him to outrun the other gazelles and to keep himself safe from the beast. The beast exists and, without your help, the slow gazelle becomes easy prey.

By the way, I was a slow gazelle. Remember when I said I wasn't a paragon of money-smart teaching? The same was true about money-smart learning. I financed my first post-college computer, a Gateway 2000 that I just *had* to have, with a credit card. I thought, "I can get a $2,000 computer, and it won't cost me *anything* now? Count me *in!*" I was clueless. In the end, I paid close to $3,000 for that computer. I did learn my lesson and never again knowingly carried a balance on a credit card. Don't be too tough on yourself when you make a mistake. It happens to us all. Keep looking forward.

[7] Thaler, Richard, and Cass Sunstein. *Nudge: Improving Decisions About Health, Wealth, and Happiness*. New York: Penguin Books, 2009.
[8] McCurrach, David. *Allowance Magic: Turn Your Kids into Money Wizards* (Franklin, TN: Kids Money Press, 2003), 6 and J14.

Memo from the Chief Mammal:
You Can't Afford
Not to Start Early

Are you ready for another serving of veggies? If not, feel free to move ahead. Otherwise...

We live in a consumer culture. When do you think kids are first exposed to media messages? Before they're two years old—sometimes when they're babies![9] Even the most progressive parents can have a difficult time keeping media out of the watchful eyes of their children. Omnipresent screens, billboards, magazines in doctors' offices and also ads in schools heighten the challenge.

Research suggests you should teach kids to be wary of consumer products and spending from a very young age—early elementary or even preschool.[10] (Please note that this instruction will not miraculously cure the "I want its" of a four-year-old. That would require actual magic dust.) By talking to your kids *early* about responsible money smarts, you expose them to messages that counter those about the consumption of *stuff.*

You may be familiar with the term "emergent literacy," the concept that children are in the process of learning to read and write by absorbing knowledge when they are in early childhood, babies even.[11] This notion is the reason many of us read to our children before they can walk.

It's helpful to consider teaching money smarts and wariness of *stuff* to young kids as "early childhood *financial* literacy," a term coined by David Godsted and Martha McCormick.[12] Young children assimilate the ever-present messages about consumption and can readily absorb communications that counter the American creed to "consume more." By *not* introducing the concepts and language of money—sharing, saving and spending **smart**—to our children at a young age, we do as much of a disservice to them as if we did not expose them early to books and writing.

---

[9] "Marketing to Children Overview." *Campaign for a Commercial-Free Childhood*, June 19, 2017, http://www.commercialfreechildhood.org/resource/marketing-children-overview.

[10] Drever, Anita I., Elizabeth Odders-White, Charles W. Kalish, Nicole M. Else-Quest, Emily M. Hoagland, and Emory N. Nelms. "Foundations of Financial Well-Being: Insights into the Role of Executive Function, Financial Socialization, and Experience-Based Learning in Childhood and Youth." *The Journal of Consumer Affairs* 49.1 (2015): 21-22. See also: Kulhmann, Eberhard. "On the Economic Analysis of the Information Seeking Behavior of Consumers." *Journal of Consumer Policy* 6.2 (1983): 231-37.

[11] McCormick, Martha H. and David Godsted. "Learning Your Monetary ABCs: The Link between Emergent Literacy and Early Childhood Financial Literacy." Networks Financial Institute at Indiana University, *NFI Report*, 2006: 3.

[12] McCormick and Godsted, "Learning Your Monetary ABCs," 8.

2

Step 1 —
The *Save* Jar

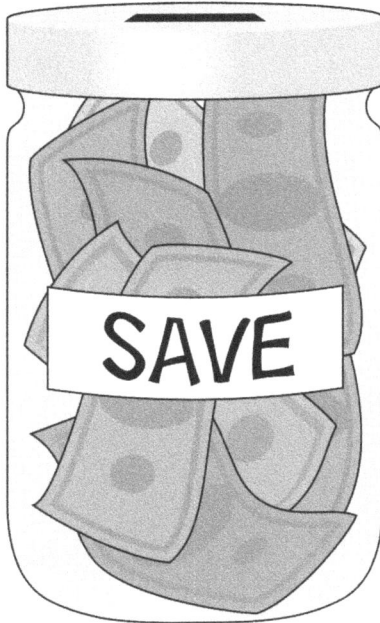

Saving for Goals

"What gets measured gets managed."

—Peter Drucker

Goals are powerful life lessons for your child. The ability to *save for a goal* is not only a core money-smart skill but also an essential *life* skill for your child to learn.

From a practical standpoint, keep your goal-setting simple. A five-year-old's attention span is short. A child's ability to visualize exists, but it's limited. Find a simple goal, like a scooter, that might take four to eight weeks of saving. Delaying gratification is okay, but not by so much that your child's eyes glaze over. Speaking of that scooter goal, our older daughter still rides around on the Razor scooter she bought when she was six.

SMART Goals

Goals should be SMART: Specific, Measurable, Achievable, Relevant and Time-based.[13] Help her decide on something she wants that is reasonably priced (specific and relevant). Identify how much your little saver intends to contribute each week

Seven years of scootering and still counting!

(time-based) and how many weeks saving for the goal will take her (measurable and achievable).

Visualization—A Simple Yet Powerful Tool

Visualization is a powerful technique employed by many individuals, from business titans to professional athletes. I've even tried to use this approach to imagine my daughters' chores getting done. Let's just say there are limitations to visualization. Yet it remains a powerful tool for helping your child save for a goal.

After helping her establish a SMART goal, print, cut out or have her draw a picture of her goal. Identify how much she's already saved—even if it's a big goose egg. Now determine how much of her allowance per week (You started that, right?) she can divert to her *Save* jar. This balance includes, but isn't limited to, whatever "opt-in" amount you've already set up.

Next, have her write down how long saving for her SMART goal will take. Depending on her age, you may need to help her with the math. Writing the date on a calendar may also be helpful. She can now paste the goal on her *Save* jar. If you prefer, you can also create and use a special savings thermometer to track progress. (See *theartofallowance.com* for materials.)

With her goal in sight, she may decide to increase her saving from the "opt-in" amount you've established. That response highlights the potential magic of saving for goals combined with methodically walking her through the process. Gentle reminders from you may not only keep her on track but also speed up the overall time-to-goal achievement.

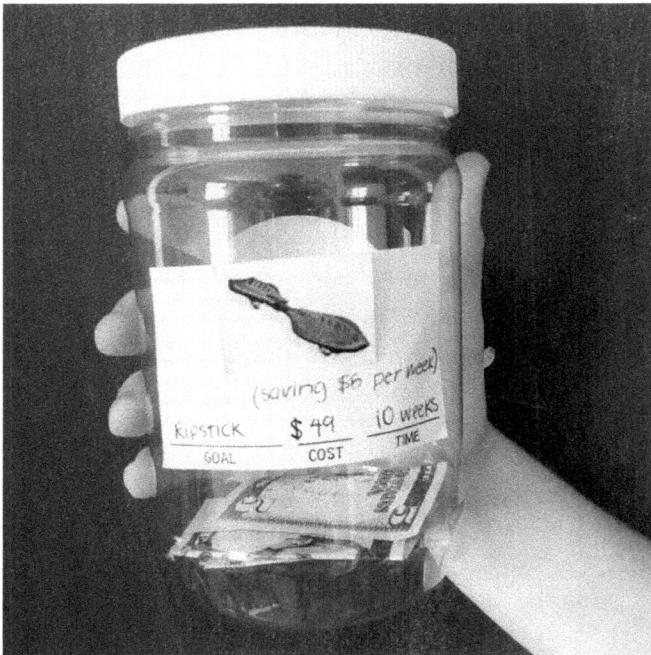

Save jar with goal on label

Brains! Yummy!

I'd like to discuss "executive function" in the brain briefly. What's that? You want to take a nap? Stay with me. A little perspective on the gray matter helps. Really.

Executive function is responsible for "inhibition," or the ability to stay on task, which is essential for any child trying to stave off temptation and save for a goal.[14] It helps him stick with savings goals, and it gives him the flexibility to deal with setbacks.

Research supports the idea that visualization—like that described above—may play a vital role in the savings process, even for a young child.[15] This analysis is why I recommend pasting the goal on the jar. That visual reminder may be what your child needs to stave off immediate temptation.

Importantly, executive function develops quickly between ages three and five, underscoring the importance of introducing financial literacy to kids earlier rather than later.[16]

Saving for More Goals

Once your child experiences success saving for her first goal, she may get the bug to save again. Or she may not. We're not in the business of driving consumption, so be patient. Just keep your ears open and eyes peeled, and an opportunity will present itself in the easy-to-recognize form of "Dad, I want..."

As for "measurable, achievable" time frames, be wary of moving your five-year-old from a short, six-week horizon on one goal to a long, six-month time frame for a follow-up goal. We actually did make the jump from an eight-week to a six-month time horizon because the *only* long-term goal our daughter wanted to save for was an American Girl doll. While I suggest smaller time increments, you're crafting your

Quinn at age five with her jars

own *Art of Allowance*. You'll soon have a sense of what your child can handle.

Our older daughter has been laser-focused since birth. Moving to a long-term goal was a good fit for her. She drifted from time to time, but she generally stayed on target with gentle reminders. If your child's horizon gets longer faster, then just remember to remind her of her goals. Visualization techniques (a goal pasted on the *Save* jar and/or the savings thermometer on the wall) help, as you can point to these methods when attention drifts. Keep the goal relevant for her. Keep her head in the game.

Trust your gut as you figure out how to help your child achieve her goals. Only you know her so well. For example, if she saved for months for a bike she wanted only to have it pilfered, then you might split the cost of a new one. I'd recommend against paying in full for the replacement item because loss happens. Dealing with it—as painful as it might be—is something she has to get used to doing.

The Waiting Period

"Dad, I have $80 in my *Save* jar, and I want my goal to be those shoes." Conveniently, those shoes are $79.99 *including* tax.

Uh oh!

It's time to invoke the "waiting period." This time-honored strategy can help your child avoid risky, impulsive decisions that she'll later regret. We have a guideline in our house that a sub-$100 goal requires the child to wait at least one week from when the decision is made (and ideally pasted on a jar). Over $100? She must wait two weeks. As usual, please adjust these guidelines to fit your family.

By the way, it's never too early for any of us to take time to think before we buy *stuff*. Why not opt both your child and yourself into the *waiting period*? It's a great way to avoid the accumulation of *stuff*.

On Control

Much of the allowance and money-smart process requires you to cede control of the money you've given your child. This act can be tough to carry out. We can guide her ("How about one gumball and not the family-size jug of Twizzlers?"), and we can restrict her ("I know it's your money, but you can't have the *Nightmare on Elm Street* sticker book. You know the family guidelines.").

In the end, your goal is to help her make money-smart choices so she eventually becomes money-empowered. She will make mistakes. That's part of the process. Making a small error now—and learning from it—is better than making a massive, more consequential mistake later. Choosing to purchase a My Colorful Unicorn set (actual name not used to protect the not-so-innocent) and seeing two weeks later that it's bald and hornless starts to build perspective about the impermanence of *stuff*. You're helping her to think about her choices, to "opt-in" to money-smart behaviors and to build good habits early. This outcome is much easier than having to break bad habits later.

Incentivizing and Matching

The "incentivizing" strategy is a key element for nudging, or getting your child to "opt-in" to beneficial behaviors as discussed earlier. If you want to see more of something, incentivize it.

The *Save* jar is the first place to start. To "nudge," give your child a quarter for every dollar she puts into her *Save* jar. This system is akin to a matching program that an employer might provide and underscores the idea that she can get paid to save. You don't need to bang her over the head with this concept. Capitalize on teaching moments. At allowance time, mention that her matching funds will help her reach her goal sooner. Thanks go again to David McCurrach's *Allowance Magic: Turn Your Kids into Money Wizards* workbook for the matching framework.[17]

We've had success in our family with the idea of *incentivizing* (or subsidizing) purchases of which we've heartily approved. As I mentioned at the beginning of the book, we wanted our kids to read more, so we agreed to pay 50% of the cost of any book. Maybe your child wants to save for a bigger item like a computer and asks you to pay half the cost. Reasonable enough. Just be sure you decide on the exact computer and price *before* you agree to contribute to her goal. What behaviors would you like to incentivize? Be sure to add them to your plan.

Enhanced Interest

In *The First National Bank of Dad,* David Owen offers the ingenious idea of paying an interest of 5 percent (or higher) per *month* so that "the miracle of compounding [is] obvious to the child."[18] In addition to matching money he drops into the *Save* jar, consider an interest rate which might actually incentivize him to save.

Because *institutional* interest rates (via credit unions, thrift institutions and banks) are generally low, an "enhanced interest" rate will have a much quicker, more visible impact on your child.

Wait a Second! What About Chores?

If you've researched allowance prior to picking up this book, then you're likely familiar with the hullabaloo about whether parents should tie allowance to chores. Opinions abound.

Karyn Hodgens, a youth money expert, elegantly describes the reasoning behind decoupling chores and allowance in her essay "Motivation Theory Applied to the Allowance/Chore Debate." (See *theartofallowance.com* for the entire essay.)

I agree with Hodgens' basic logic. Though paying a child for chores can teach him that money comes from work—a valuable lesson—allowance is more effectively used as a money-empowerment tool. By providing him an allowance with money he mostly controls and by giving him proper parental guidance and nudging, he can learn the three core skills: *making smart money choices, distinguishing needs from wants* and *saving for goals.* He will learn to handle money as a tool—including making mistakes with *actual* money—on his way to becoming money-smart and money-empowered.

He does basic chores, such as clearing the table or making his bed, because you're raising a responsible member of the household. You can teach him the link between hard work and money—a different lesson than the one afforded by allowance—by giving him what Hodgens calls "Above-and-Beyond Jobs." These tasks, like mowing the lawn or cleaning the car, are jobs that you might pay someone else to do.[19] Of course, what's "basic" and what's "Above-and-Beyond" will differ from family to family. Again, the *art*.

Motivation theory teaches us that allowance, when not controlled by chores, is controlled by your child. Via intrinsic motivation, essentially self-motivation, your child is exerting his own power over the choices from which he will learn. The control is in his hands.

Extrinsic motivation—driven by external factors—has consistently been shown to have decreasing motivational power the longer those outside rewards are used. Kids (and adults) become desensitized to extrinsic motivation.[20]

Some individuals argue that an allowance not tied to chores is akin to an entitlement.[21] That belief assumes accountability only comes from working for money. Of course, just giving him some money and calling it an allowance *is* an entitlement. Granting him a purposeful allowance with a plan as described here is *not* a handout.

There will be time for him to learn the lesson that money can come from work, but the primary purpose of an allowance is to teach him to become a responsible user of money as a tool. When you *intentionally* craft your own *Art of Allowance* using strategies identified in this book, you turn money into a teaching tool.

One additional benefit which Hodgens doesn't mention is that decoupling chores and allowance helps reduce money negativity. As any parent who assigns chores knows, they often lead to conflict. This negativity inevitably spills into money conversations. If your kids do chores as ours do, then you can probably relate to this fun exchange:

"Honey, it's time to clean the dishes."

Her eyes protrude.

The blood drains from her face.

Her mouth opens. "Nooooooooooo!"

With allowance and chores intertwined, this exchange likely devolves into a money threat: "If you don't do your chores, then you're *not* getting paid!" When possible, we should try to *limit* money negativity. Money conversations are already often burdened by persistent societal taboos that promote silence about the green stuff. These taboos are fed by negativity, which is fueled by many issues, including the embarrassment about our own use of money, the guilt of having too much or the desperation of not having enough. By tying chores and allowance together, you're setting the stage for more money conflict. Decoupling can help change this outcome.

So, are you wrong to tie chores to allowance? Not necessarily. There are some authorities who think chores must accompany allowance. The case is not closed. In fact, there are researchers who question an allowance in general.[22] If you feel uncomfortable providing your child an allowance without tying it to chores, then tie away.

My opinion on this issue has evolved over time. I now believe that your giving an allowance to and beginning a money dialogue with your child are more important than my trying to convince you that decoupling allowance and chores is the better path. Whatever you decide, remember, choosing some form of allowance is important. Without real money, teaching money smarts is just an abstraction.

[13] Lawlor, K. Blaine and Martin J. Hornyak. "Smart Goals: How the Application of Smart Goals Can Contribute to Achievement of Student Learning Outcomes." *Developments in Business Simulation and Experiential Learning* 39 (2012): 259-67.

[14] Drever et al., "Foundations," 15.

[15] Holden, Karen, Charles Kalish, Laura Scheinholtz, Deanna Dietrich, and Beatriz Novak. "Financial Literacy Programs Targeted on Pre-School Children: Development and Evaluation." Working Paper 2009-009. Washington, DC: Credit Union National Association (CUNA), 2009.

[16] Moore, Chris, Karen Lemmon, and Karen Skene. *The Self in Time: Developmental Perspectives.* Mahwah, NJ: Psychology Press, 2001.

[17] McCurrach, *Allowance Magic*, 7.

[18] Owen, David. *The First National Bank of Dad: The Best Way to Teach Kids About Money* (New York: Simon & Schuster, 2003), 18-20.

[19] Hodgens, Karyn. "Motivation Theory Applied to the Allowance/Chore Debate." *Kidnexions,* September 2010, http://kidnexions.com/pdf/MotivationTheoryAppliedtotheAllowance.pdf.

[20] Pink, Daniel. *Drive: The Surprising Truth About What Motivates Us* (New York: Penguin Group, 2011), 34-37.

[21] Kadlec, Dan. "Why Giving Your Kids an Allowance May Not Teach Them Anything." *TIME,* February 15, 2012, http://business.time.com/2012/02/15/why-giving-your-kids-an-allowance-might-not-be-teaching-them-anything/.

[22] Mandell, Lewis. "Child Allowances – Beneficial or Harmful?" *Lewis Mandell, Ph.D.*, August 12, 2017, http://lewismandell.com/child_allowances_-_beneficial_or_harmful

Memo from the Chief Mammal:
The Power of Money Taboos

*"For there is nothing either good or
bad, but thinking makes it so."*
—*Hamlet*

Many of our money taboos are deep-seated.

I recently had lunch with a friend. We went out for
sushi, and he wanted to order family-style. Sharing. I
don't mind family-style eating as long as everyone's
style is mine.

I'm a bit of a sushi purist. I don't like any crazy rolls.
My friend ordered two of them, neither of which
appealed to me. Instead of saying, "I'll just order the
lunch special, sushi," which would have saved me $15
and been more delicious, I went with the flow. I didn't
want to come off as cheap. (This conviction is one of
my baked-in taboos.) And I'm 48 years old! Grow up,
Chief Mammal!

No doubt, my friend would have been perfectly fine
with my choice. My personal taboo was 100 percent
of the problem.

We all need to come to terms with our taboos
and address them head-on, lest we hold on to
them too long and pass them on to our children.
Taking a moment to take stock of what your money
taboos are—and how you can overcome them—is

worthwhile in helping you gain perspective when speaking with your kids.

3
—

Step 2 —
The *Spend Smart* Jar

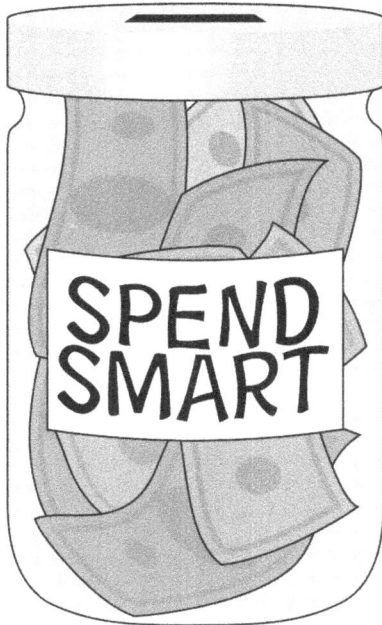

More Than Words

"Becoming is better than being."

—*Carol Dweck*

"You should add 'Smart' to ALL the jars," a friend of mine chided me. "You're right," I said, "but try singing, 'We'll Share Smart, Save Smart and Spend Smart Too!'" Marbles in the mouth. (Watch *The Money Mammals* theme song at *theartofallowance.com*.) And really, spending is often the most frivolous action. After all, they don't call those who save a lot *savethrifts!*

Getting kids to associate smarts with spending may appear to be just a semantic, trivial gesture, but it is a big deal. The sooner, the better. You can introduce this connection when your children are *very* young. *Thrive by Five*, a website by the Credit Union National Association, is no longer live, but it used to offer up some good two-page activities. I've detailed some strategies below in that spirit which we've used with our kids.

Smart Trips

You can take your three- or four-year-old to the store and give him a dollar to spend. Tell him he can get anything in the store. Work through the price tags with him. You'll have to drive the conversation, and don't worry about his having a complete understanding of the purchasing process by the time you're finished. "That bicycle is a little more than one dollar, son. Let's try the dollar section for something that might work better." Help him pick out an item, pay for it, and receive change. This act helps him start to understand how money works. You're working on the *early childhood financial literacy* concept I detailed earlier.

On your next trip to the store, incorporate a lesson about *distinguishing needs from wants*. Explain that eating breakfast is a need, but a bowl of sugared cereal is a want. Talk to him about why carrots might be a need (if your kid, like our younger daughter, considers carrots the *only* edible vegetable) and why a seven-layer chocolate cake is a want.

Not All *Stuff* Is Created Equal

I mentioned before that our daughter *really* wanted an American Girl doll. She saved passionately for months to buy the doll that cost over $100 (with tax). She would not be denied. We also used the opportunity as a math lesson, requiring her to sort and bag all the coins and dollars to make things as easy as possible on the cashier. The transaction went well, and she was thrilled. As a bonus, her grandmother even sent her the doll's bed for Christmas.

Eventually, it dawned on her that she wasn't really a doll person. The sheen had worn off. With our help, she sold the doll on eBay for about $20.

This experience stands in stark contrast to the My Colorful Unicorn set she purchased with her *Spend Smart* money. She lost interest in that item almost before we returned home from the shopping trip. This incident, in part, led to our adopting the *waiting period* detailed earlier.

Some purchases of *stuff* are passion projects, and some transactions are just silly. Use your best judgement about how and

Bagged coins: I was impressed with the cashier's patience with this transaction.

when to make that point. Be explicit when that item she "had to have" is forgotten. Your child is unlikely to respond with, "Gosh, Dad, you're so right," but she will no doubt remember the experience.

Think back to all the *stuff* you've purchased to give you some perspective on the time these lessons take to sink in fully. Think about the head start you're giving her! You're teaching her that *stuff* provides only fleeting excitement, and she's learning this lesson through her own experience. Powerful.

Magic Money

Electronic transactions can seem *magical*. Demystify these transactions by using the *actual* green stuff. Consider using cash for your transactions on some of *your* trips to the market. Your son's experience seeing real money exchanges is beneficial. Talk him through each transaction with a focus on familiarity rather than on full comprehension. There are important life lessons to be learned—like you can't buy a bike for a dollar.

Hidden Choices

Encourage your child to learn about choices by talking him through the choices *you* make, which will undoubtedly be educational for him. Talk to him about your decision, for example, to buy a more economical car instead of a high-performance machine.

These *hidden choices* can be explained. He sees you lay down thousands of dollars for a car and claim you're spending smart while advising him not to buy another twenty-dollar building block set. If you don't explain your hidden choices, then can you blame him if he gives you the same look my wife gives me when I tell her *The Voice* is frivolous while I sit down to watch my beloved Seattle Seahawks for three hours?

Memo from the Chief Mammal:

Thriving, Happy People

*"Much of society equates
self-worth with net worth."*
—James Altucher

I am hopeful we have an opportunity to become a country more focused on happiness than wealth. By that, I mean happiness in the larger sense: thriving, fulfilling, flourishing. I'm optimistic we can define ourselves more commonly by our beliefs and the value we provide to society rather than by *stuff*.

Fringe ideas and institutions, like the Gross Happiness Index and the Center for a New American Dream, that are moving mainstream are encouraging. These visions balance the outsized importance of Gross Domestic Product and the "American Dream," focused on things, with feelings of well-being and fulfillment. Remembering that our founding fathers believed "the pursuit of happiness"—happiness in the larger sense—to be one of our "unalienable rights" is instructive.

When I mention this vision to parents, I'll often get "skeptical face" in return. You know, the expression you get when your angriest friend insists you listen to his transformative self-help audio.

I get it. When we are in the throes of parenting and see our kids bewitched by brands, this shiny, happy vision I have sounds more distant than our chance to live in a galaxy far, far away. But I believe it may be coming.

Yet challenges to this vision surround us. We're here for a substantially short time. If saying that no one on his deathbed ever wished he'd worked more is cliché, then why do so many Americans continue to work themselves to the bone? Hyperconnectedness (*Facebook, Twitter,* email) certainly contributes to this attitude, as does our inability to say "no."

Fortunately, awareness of this problem is growing. Many of us are beginning to move from the pursuit of *stuff* to "the pursuit of happiness" for ourselves and for our families. Though they are certainly not for everyone, fringe movements like "Minimalism" are gaining traction, and they underscore this point. And though having only fifteen worldly possessions is not for everyone, more of us are saying 'yes' to what we believe is good for our well being and 'no' to what isn't. *That* gives me hope and is one reason I wrote this book—to try to make a small contribution to this transition.

4

—

Step 3 —
The *Share* Jar

The Family Plan

"I want to play with Charity. She has all my toys."

—Quinn Lanza

Our daughter actually uttered this statement. On our way back from the donation center where we had donated a big bag of her old toys, our then three-year-old innocently peered at me in the mirror and shared her desire. We had instituted our family plan to combat the accumulation of *stuff*. For every new birthday present received, one old item had to go. This practice satisfied both my inner Marie Kondo and our limited-space issue.

Our daughter didn't necessarily understand our approach. Her concern underscores the idea that we want to expose our kids to important concepts, yet we have to be wary of taking things too far. In our house, mindfulness of *stuff* has become a kind of religion, and sometimes I spend a little too much time in church.

You may discover that saving for goals and spending smart tend to be top of mind with your child because kids are primarily want-based. The *Share* jar is different. We "opt-in" kids to charitable giving because we believe regular donations of money and time are good for the community and for our general sense of well-being. Of course, because the *Share* jar isn't want-based like the *Save* and *Spend Smart* jars, you may need to draw attention to it actively as opportunities arise.

Sharing at School

Your kids' schools are always asking for money. Well, at least my children's schools are. Have your son contribute to his education by participating in his school's annual fundraising campaign.

Be on the lookout for ways he can donate his money at school. High-profile disasters—such as Hurricane Sandy or the Japanese tsunami—often result in school-generated relief efforts, which are exemplary opportunities for your child to donate. Even if your child genuinely appreciates the opportunity to make a donation, he might still need a little encouragement to remember to use his *Share* jar money to help others.

Online Donations

Donation opportunities may be found online. For example, *DonorsChoose.org* is a well-run charity that helps teachers and schools raise needed funds. Your child may be able to help local schools, possibly even his own. If you decide to go the online route, then sit down with him, and look at the different opportunities. When you process the transactions—assuming he hasn't graduated to the Breakthrough Allowance detailed later—have him give you the cash, and walk through the online exchange while he watches.

UNICEF

You walk into your seven-year-old daughter's room and

distribute her allowance. She puts two "opt-in" dollars into the *Save* jar and four discretionary dollars into the *Spend Smart* jar. (Of course, the four dollars could alternatively go into the *Save* or *Share* jars instead.) She drops one more "opt-in" dollar into the *Share* jar.

You then notice she's accumulated *twenty-two dollars* in her *Share* jar. Wow! Now you need to figure out something to do with that money. Breathe easy. Even if you remember the *Share* jar only once a year, make sure you do so the week before Halloween. All kidding aside, the ubiquitous UNICEF box is as good a place as any for your daughter to put at least some of her *Share* money. (See *theartofallowance.com* for more resources.)

Making Charity Personal

The lack of attention that we were paying to the *Share* jars in our own house was a problem, so I took my own advice. Rather than dwell on yet another parenting miscue, I was inspired to write my second *Money Mammals* children's book, *Joe the Monkey Learns to Share.*

In the book, our intrepid star, Joe the Monkey, can't find a charity to which he wants to donate, so he starts his own. If you have an entrepreneurial kid with a desire to help others in his *own* way, then support his effort to make sharing more personal. Whether he's using the *Share* jar money to build homeless kits or collecting money and items for a children's hospital, this personal touch can be an empowering way for him to use those funds.

Gotcha!

In my first children's book, *Joe the Monkey Saves for a Goal,* Joe's little sister, Marmoset, takes money from her *Share* jar to help her older brother save for the new Supervine 3000 he craves. My intention in the book was that Marmoset's gift to Joe would be a selfless gesture to help her brother—one worthy of the *Share* jar money. This fictional tale, however, came back to bite me like a vengeful monkey when our daughters colluded to use my words against me.

Our older daughter was saving for an item she claimed she was planning to share with her sister. It was something along the lines of a My Colorful Unicorn set. I blocked the exchange by saying it wasn't a proper use of *Share* jar money. She promptly pulled *my* book off the shelf and showed me Joe's little sister, Marmoset, emptying her *Share* jar to help her older brother. Touché! I capitulated, respecting her ingenuity.

Flexible *guidelines* in your *art*—versus hard-and-fast *rules*—will allow you to make important judgment calls like this one along the way. Still, I generally wouldn't recommend the use of *Share* jar funds in this way. The money should go directly to a legitimate cause.

5

Tweens, Teens and the Breakthrough Allowance

The Annual Review

"Confidence comes from repetition."

—*Debbie Millman*

As your child gets older, you'll want to increase her allowance to reflect her ability, hopefully, to handle larger amounts of money. Doing so on an annual basis, like on her birthday, is straightforward. You could, for example, give your seven-year-old another dollar per week and take the opportunity to review her allowance program:

- Maybe it's time to increase the "opt-in" amounts for the *Share* jar to go to charitable contributions.

- Maybe it's time to "opt-in" more money to the *Save* jar for those longer-term wants.

- Maybe the increase in allowance should be another discretionary dollar that reflects your trust in her growing ability to make decisions on her own (my recommendation).

- Maybe you also want to alter any *incentive* or *matching* programs you have in place.

You'll want to revisit the reasons she's receiving an allowance—to learn to be responsible with and smart about money. You can emphasize the core skills again. With the increased allowance, you can share your expectation to see even smarter spending, saving and sharing. Remind her that she's getting an allowance to become money-smart. Even if the reminder feels a little forced or awkward, it is important. *This money is not a handout.* This conversation is a part of the allowance process and a learning tool for her.

It's also a good time to take a look at the *Share* and *Save* jars to see if she can find a charitable cause to which to donate or a goal toward which she might like to save.

Tweens and Teens

By the time your child becomes a tween or a teenager, he has hopefully saved for several SMART goals. He has been making money choices regularly by putting his allowance into the *Share, Save* and *Spend Smart* jars. He will also have been receiving increased allowances each year commensurate with his rising maturity level. He's feeling money-smart and slowly becoming money-empowered.

Why, then, does he look at you with such disdain? Because that's what tweens do. And they're good at it. The warm and fuzzy days of jars may now be coming to an end, but you've provided him with a pretty solid money foundation. And *this* is what you get in return? Raising kids is a bit like dollar-cost averaging—steady investment through the highs and lows will pay off.

Our older daughter—now a teenager—is almost always negotiating with me. She was recently developing an expensive açaí bowl habit that we didn't want to feed. In a moment of my weakness, she convinced me to take her to Jamba Juice, where she would typically be responsible for the purchase using her new Breakthrough Allowance that I will explain shortly. I picked her up from track practice, and she looked so spent that I agreed to buy her a smoothie. Using my acquiescence as a beachhead, she launched her full-scale assault for the pricier item, begging, "Can I pleeeeease have an açaí bowl?" (Nagging or begging, which *The Art of Allowance* can help reduce, is like a horror movie villain. It never really seems to die.) I told her no, unless she wanted to cover the difference. She didn't and enjoyed her smoothie. (In case you're wondering, I don't always prevail in these negotiations.)

Eventually, your tween or teen will advance to what I call the "Breakthrough Allowance." As he moves from childhood toward adulthood, you want to help him become more responsible with more money. The way you distribute the money and his increased responsibilities should make him feel more like an adult. Again, be explicit about what you're doing. You can tell him that both he and his allowance are growing up.

You want to continue to help your child improve at the core skills and to recognize better the impermanent excitement that *stuff* brings. *More* money and *bigger* things don't change this feeling! If you haven't already, you may even introduce *investment* into the mix.

None of these tasks will be simple. Nothing involving a teenager ever is. But with a plan and a commitment to raising a money-smart kid, you can help him break through to become a money-empowered young adult.

The Breakthrough Allowance

Your tween or teen is now ready for the Breakthrough

Allowance, a major developmental step. She's moving past the starter allowance detailed earlier. Her responsibilities will increase substantially. She'll create a yearly spending plan, and her allowance intervals will change. You may even decide to incorporate a digital allowance as I explain below.

Since she is "graduating" from her starter allowance, a little celebration might be in order. Before she embarks on the next stage of this journey, commend her for the progress she's made in learning the three core money-smart skills: *saving for goals, making smart money choices* and *distinguishing needs from wants.* Let her know this step is a meaningful milestone.

There are some obvious areas of responsibility for your burgeoning money maven: clothes, communication, gifts and food. Don't let the "food" category scare you. I'm talking about bringing versus buying school lunch, not raising her own farm animals. (Although that undertaking would certainly teach her responsibility.)

You'll be increasing her total allowance amount substantially to accommodate for these new areas of control. The additional responsibilities of clothes, communication, gifts and food all belong in the *Spend Smart* domain. This time is a good one to consider using a digital allowance like the options offered via *FamZoo* or *FamilyMint.* (Links are available at *theartofallowance.com.*)

A digital allowance enables you to automate the allowance distribution process into virtual "jars." You can also automate interest and matching. Part of her progression to becoming money-empowered is learning how to become digitally money-smart. Though a digital allowance simplifies the process, automation is silent, and you'll want to make sure you continue the money conversation with your child.

I suggest you continue to nudge or mandate an "opt-in" to the *Share* and *Save* jars (real or virtual). You may decide to give her free reign, but with the increase in responsibility, keeping those nudges in place is probably a good idea. In fact, if you employ a digital allowance, then you can teach her the power of automatic deposits into *Share* and *Save* accounts so that she never sees— and isn't tempted by—the money in her discretionary *Spend Smart* account.

Also, the overall *percentage* of the *Share* and *Save* "opt-in" contributions will likely go down, as she'll be controlling much more discretionary income with the Breakthrough Allowance. Of course, it's your *Art of Allowance*, and you may mandate larger chunks of money for either the *Share* or *Save* jars or for both.

Clothes

Giving your child control of clothes purchasing as soon as you can is beneficial. You'll be shocked (unless you already have a teen) at how quickly her friends' opinions will impact her life. Without a plan, a clothing decision swiftly becomes something for which adult input is *not* solicited—*until* the time comes to swipe the credit card.

Transferring clothing responsibility to your child helps stave off nagging for twenty bucks here and thirty bucks there. More importantly, your child then has *skin in the game* and will more thoughtfully consider her purchases. I think you'll find implementing this plan will *save* you significant money in the long run.

I wish we'd tracked spending for clothes, communication, gifts and food leading up to the Breakthrough Allowance. I'd love to say we knew exactly how much she should budget per month on clothes. But we didn't. I tip my cap to those parents who do.

We *did* sit down with our twelve-year-old at the start of the Breakthrough Allowance process to help her work through the proper monthly amount, using a spreadsheet which I created from her yearly spending plan.

If you're looking for a helpful workbook to further walk you through this process, David McCurrach's *Allowance Magic: Turn Your Kids into Money Wizards* is excellent. (The link is available at *theartofallowance.com*.)

Communication

If and when (okay, *when*) you decide your child should have a phone, she should at least pay her portion of the monthly bill. This practice is particularly easy to do if you're using an automated digital allowance.

My wife and I typically gift our hand-me-down phones to our daughters. Some folks have their kids pay a nominal amount for used phones. Your choice. Interestingly, our older daughter would wait as long as possible to get a free phone. Though she's more of a natural spender than her sister, she wanted to direct her money to other *stuff* she really cared about. And yes, she's still learning about the impermanence of the "jolt" that *stuff* brings. Building this knowledge base takes time.

Our younger daughter, a more natural saver, decided she wanted a newer, faster, pricier phone with a good camera and saved for it using *Save* jar funds. However, she did buy a refurbished one to save herself some money.

Gifts

Adding gifts for friends to your daughter's responsibility basket is sensible. This practice forces her to think—yep, *Spend **Smart***—about her own gifting. Watching this change in perspective is funny. Once our daughter became the one forking out the gift money, she decided that good enough was okay.

When your child is responsible for buying gifts, they become generally more meaningful. Frankly, we all know what happens to a kid's creative gift idea when she realizes you'll cave and take her to Brandy Melville in the 11th hour. Adiós, plan! When the money is coming out of *her* pocket—or jar—a light bulb goes off. She becomes the Martha Stewart of gifting.

Food

One of the best pieces of advice offered in Ron Lieber's terrific book *The Opposite of Spoiled: Raising Kids Who Are Grounded, Generous, and Smart About Money* is to have your child make his own lunch.[23] If you want to improve your family's morning routine, then try this trick. It works wonders!

We made a deal with our kids—we'd buy lunch fixin's at no cost to them. The decision whether to bring lunch or buy it at school with their Breakthrough Allowances was theirs. This system serves as an incentive against blowing money on too many school lunches—which can add up. We also included money for after-school snacks on the local boulevard with friends. These relatively small expenses can add up fast, so make sure to try to account for as many of them as possible when you negotiate the Breakthrough Allowance with your teen or tween.

I don't, however, recommend going cold turkey and budgeting nothing for school lunches. When you first set up the Breakthrough Allowance, you'll want your child to allocate money for a few school lunches per month. You'll need a safety valve on those "special" mornings when your child has a meltdown, and absolutely no lunch is forthcoming. It's only a matter of time. Be prepared!

On Budgeting

I have a secret—one I've already partially revealed. I'm not a big budget guy. This reality exists largely because I've always had difficulty sticking to a formal plan. My wife and I find reviewing spending patterns and being mindful about our spending and saving more useful.

If you *are* a budgeter, then fantastic! The Breakthrough Allowance helps your child learn basic budgeting. (See the spreadsheet below.) You can show him how you keep your spending under control—whether via budgeting, tracking spending or both. By sharing your strategies, you will help him to discover what method works best for him and to become more mindful of his own spending habits.

Change the Frequency

When you transition to the Breakthrough Allowance, I suggest switching from a weekly or biweekly allowance payment to a monthly arrangement. Receiving chunks of money is more akin to what happens in the real world. This practice will let her experience that start-of-the-month feeling of being flush with cash (like her "paycheck" just cleared). If she blows her "windfall" early in the month, then let her feel the pain. As hard as this endeavor might be, she needs to learn this life lesson. Let her struggle to manage her money better. Don't bail her out.

You have flexibility in making the leap from the basic *one-dollar-per-week-per-age-of-your-child* allowance to the new Breakthrough Allowance. And if you're worried that going "all in" with the four categories is too much for your particular child, then start with one area—gifts, for instance. Or if you feel comfortable that she's ready to make the breakthrough and tackle more responsibility, then pile on the challenge. Here's an example of the simple spreadsheet I created with our oldest daughter when we negotiated her Breakthrough Allowance to be $125 per month. (See *theartofallowance.com*.)

Be prepared—and proud—when the spreadsheet becomes a negotiation. She will be feeling more money-empowered than when you started her on this money-smart journey. You *want* her to negotiate the best possible deal for herself—another great life skill for her to learn.

Our daughter originally came to us with an allocation of $25 for each birthday present. We felt that amount was too high, and we ended up at what we believed was a more reasonable $20 per present. When the final monthly amount came to $124, she "rounded" that number to the nearest five and asked for $125 a month "for fairness." Maybe I'm a sucker, but her creative thinking for an extra twelve bucks per year worked on me. (Hmm…I sense a theme.) I really don't know what she meant by "fairness" here, but her reasoning made me chuckle. She was probably still trying to make up for her perceived post-negotiation gift deficit.

As you did with the starter allowance, you'll want to set up a periodic review of the Breakthrough Allowance on an annual or biannual basis.

NEGOTIATING BREAKTHROUGH ALLOWANCE			
Categories	Negotiations	Yearly Totals	Monthy Allowance
Clothes	$10/mo. x 12 mos.	$120	$10
Communication	$15/mo. x 12 mos.	$180	$15
Gifts	$20/birthday x 20 birthdays	$400	$33
Food	$10/school lunch x 5 per month = $50 mo. x 12 mos.	$600	$50
Spend Smart			$108
Save	$10/mo. x 12 mos.	$120	$10
Share	$6/mo. x 12 mos	$72	$6
Sub-Total			$124
For Fairness			1
TOTAL			$125

Quinn's Breakthrough Allowance Spreadsheet

Opening a Savings Account & Gift Money

There's never a bad time to open a savings account for your child in a credit union, thrift institution or bank. In fact, you should take this step well before establishing the Breakthrough Allowance, and you should bring your child along when you open the account. Explain that you and your partner keep your money in a savings account for safekeeping.

You can also explain the concept of interest at a bank or dividends at a credit union—the amount the institution pays you to hold your money. If you're employing *enhanced interest*, a practice by which you pay your child an interest rate to encourage saving, then you can tell him that this concept is basically the same thing. However, the rate in a credit union, thrift institution or bank is bound to be lower.

The savings account is also a good place to deposit large money gifts if your child is fortunate enough to receive them. Some relatives' gifts may go beyond what you're willing to let your child control (particularly when he's younger). If your child has a savings account, then half the funds could be deposited in that account, and the balance could go to the child's *Share, Save* or *Spend Smart* jars!

You can also conspire—as we did—with his grandparents to have them send three bills, each marked with the appropriate jar—*Share, Save* and *Spend Smart.* (Cue wicked laughter.)

You may be thinking, "But you said not to hide money from the kids." Our strategy is to empower our kids with money in hand—an allowance. Making money less available to use is a time-honored and sensible long-term saving strategy that works for many adults. Of course, with older kids, be upfront with the split. For example, tell your child the family guideline for large money gifts is that he gets half the money, and the rest goes into his savings account. Or you might put the entire amount in your child's savings account. Your choice.

Investing

I am not a professional investor, and me giving you investment advice would be a little like Colonel Sanders giving you advice on healthy eating. Like any investor, I have had my share of ups and downs and am now basically in index funds. You may be an expert investor and may want to pass that skill along to your child. Make it part of your *Art of Allowance.* There are plenty of publications on investing. This book is not one of them.

I do, however, have some thoughts on how to *introduce* your child to investing. Consider setting up an investment account for your child, or let her piggy back on your investments. She can purchase some shares of a stock by examining companies that are personally meaningful. Our older daughter, an athlete, bought Adidas stock. She's had fun with the investment. (Who wouldn't? It went up!) She considered selling it until we told her she'd have to pay our short-term tax rate. We suggested she hold it for at least a year and pay the much lower long-term capital gains tax rate. We explained the risk associated with holding onto the stock and measured that chance against the tax implications of selling now. Investing was a good learning experience, and we broke what is often a money conversation taboo—the reluctant parent's unwillingness to discuss the topic because of past debacles.

You can also set up an automated allowance deduction to an index fund, so she can start to learn the power of compound interest at an early age. You may want to post a compound interest graph somewhere in the house to expose her to the power of the time value of money. (See *theartofallowance.com.*)

In short, you can help your child see the value of compound interest far sooner than when I learned of it from my money-empowered Granddad.

Encouraging your child to dabble in stock gives her a sense of how companies offer stock to obtain money to grow. She can learn how she as a stockholder can own a small part of a company and make or lose money depending on the company's performance. By introducing her to index funds and setting up an automatic deduction, you help nudge or "opt-in" your child to a choice—investing in her future—that could make a huge difference for her down the road.

If It's Good Enough for the Oracle of Omaha...

Renowned investment guru Warren Buffett (aka the "Oracle of Omaha") noted in a *New York Times* article that when he dies, he wants his investments put into index funds and government bonds. Why not in stocks? He said he's known only *ten* people who have consistently beaten the stock market.[24] (I'm guessing that one of those ten individuals is his partner, Charlie Munger.) That statement should give us amateurs pause. Index funds and governments bonds are less risky investments that provide opportunities for growth. If they are good enough for the Oracle of Omaha...

Your Kids May Shock You

Here's a little story I have to share with you. Our older daughter saved for and purchased a new GoPro camera from Amazon. She headed off to the beach with my wife and her little sister. Then the text came in.

Wife: The camera is gone.

Me: Seriously?

Wife: It gets worse.

Me: Why? Anyone hurt?

Wife: Her sister dropped it in the water.

Me: Oh my! (This exclamation, translated from the profane, was not really what I said to myself.)

The little sister lost the new camera *within an hour* of trying it out for the first time. (Why do you find out about the little floaty thing you attach to the GoPro *after* the camera sinks to the bottom of the Pacific?)

Then something amazing happened. The little sister agreed to take the money from her own *Save* jar to give to her distraught sibling to replace the lost camera. Now, I know one could argue that this move was borne of self-preservation, but higher-level, money-smart thinking was also at work. Our daughter used money appropriately as a tool to atone for her mistake. As one familiar with first-child thinking, I'm not sure the sentiment would have been reciprocated had the roles been reversed. Regardless, we were proud of the little sister's choice.

The way *you* deal with a situation like this one might be different. You may decide to cover half the cost of the replacement GoPro to help out your daughter. Again, your *art,* your choice. We thought the life lesson was more valuable if our younger daughter followed through with her replacement offer.

Of course, we're not completely heartless—we did buy that little floaty thing for the new GoPro.

---

23 Lieber, Ron. *The Opposite of Spoiled: Raising Kids Who Are Grounded, Generous, and Smart About Money* (New York: Harper Collins, 2015), 155-57.
24 Sorkin, Andrew Ross. "Buffett Asks Big Money: Why Pay High Fees?" *The New York Times,* February 27, 2017, https://www.nytimes.com/2017/02/27/business/dealbook/buffett-asks-big-money-why-pay-high-fees.html.

Memo from the Chief Mammal:
Wanting More?

*"The more we associate experience
with cash value, the more we
think that money is what we need
to live."*

—Rolf Potts

As Seth Godin pointed out on *The Tim Ferriss Show* podcast, you have to make a choice once you have provided the basics for your family (food, shelter, healthcare and clothing)—"How much more money [do I want] and what am I going to trade for it? Because we always trade something for it." [25]

What are you willing to trade for more money? And is that money what you really want?

As I previously noted in the memo "Beware of *Stuff*," we should be wary of deluding ourselves into thinking we need more than the square feet in which we're currently living—assuming we're fortunate enough to have a home or an apartment.

Do we need a shiny new Tesla Model S because it's good for the environment? Beautiful car in my opinion, but tough to make a case for it. Want, yes. Need, no. And are we willing to trade time away from our kids for work to pay for that luxury?

Perhaps doing so may make sense if you're a car

enthusiast. Just be sure you know what you're giving up for that indulgence. More than just money might be sacrificed. Be sure you're making fully informed, conscious decisions.

Remember those *hidden choices* we discussed earlier? What messages are you sending to your kids? What are you willing to trade for your wants?

Consider doing a *stuff inventory reduction* with your family. A good starting point is Marie Kondo's KonMari method detailed in *The Life-Changing Magic of Tidying Up*.[26] Or just complete a cutback for yourself, and show your child how much *stuff* you've eliminated and donated to charity. Have your child join you at Goodwill when you make the donation. Look for an opportunity to help with her own *stuff inventory reduction*.

Research strongly suggests that kids learn by observing their parents' financial behavior.[27] Accumulation of *stuff* is a financial behavior of which we need to be aware. It has an impact.

---

[25] "How Seth Godin Manages His Life-Rules, Principles, and Obsessions." *The Tim Ferriss Show with Tim Ferriss*. *The Tim Ferriss Blog*, February 10, 2016, https://tim.blog/2016/02/10/seth-godin/.
[26] Kondo, Marie. *The Life-Changing Magic of Tidying Up: The Japanese Art of Decluttering and Organizing*. Berkeley: Ten Speed Press, 2014.
[27] Drever et al., "Foundations," 21-22. See also: Ward, Scott, Daniel Wackman, and Ellen Wartella. "The Development of Consumer Information-Processing Skills: Integrating Cognitive Development and Family Interaction Theories." *Advances in Consumer Research* 4 (1977): 166-71.

6
—

An Important Question, Mindsets and More

What if My Kid Is Too Old?

"Failure is an event—never a person!"

—William D. Brown

Q. I have a ten-year-old son, and we haven't started teaching him about money. Is all hope lost?

A. First, relax. There is plenty of hope. Although beginning early is better, your starting at age ten puts you ahead of *a lot* of folks. Beginning can seem like a daunting task. Unlike the wide-eyed five-year-old, a tween is entering the "my parents are marginally smarter than an amoeba" phase. *Triple* that disdain for a teenager.

You might be surprised by your child though. One mom, concerned how her tween would react, approached the allowance start-up with some trepidation. Below was her email after the initial discussion:

> P.S., picked her up today, she was sullen and closed off, "How was your day?" Greeted with, "Awful. How do you think?"
>
> I took her out for tacos, suggested the plan being hatched re allowance and she responded by saying

she'd been wanting an allowance FOREVER.

So yes, there is hope.

Think of introducing an allowance as you would teaching your child to ride a bike. A simple allowance acts as training wheels. Like the bike, if you've waited until he's ten, then he'll have more coordination than when he was seven. However, delaying the game doesn't mean he won't need assistance. Some kids might take to an allowance faster than others. Keep your eyes out for opportunities to encourage—leading him down the road to money empowerment sooner rather than later. Watch him ride. You'll know soon enough when the training wheels can come off.

You can start a ten-year-old with an allowance of ten dollars per week. You can adjust the amount up or down as you see fit, but beware of *Spendthrift Syndrome,* where you dole out a pittance because you don't trust your child with money. Remember, you want to empower your child. Start small, but not too small. Don't send him around the block on the first ride with a Breakthrough Allowance, and make sure you don't give him a bike without wheels.

Set up the three jars: *Share, Save* and *Spend Smart.* Mandate some choices to start. For example, require that he put three dollars into the *Save* jar and two into the *Share* jar. As I mention in "Getting Started," give him discretionary control of the balance—five dollars in this case—which can be put into any of the three jars.

Please don't feel like using jars is too childish. It is not. With physical jars and the techniques described previously, you can teach him the power of visualization and the core skill of *saving for goals.* You can even use the savings thermometer to track his progress.

You may have started late, but there's still no rush. We don't want him to lose perspective or to become overwhelmed. If he successfully saves for his first goal, then give him more control over his money (fewer nudges or "opt-ins"). Also, allow him to establish a longer time horizon for the next goal. Slow and steady.

Not sure how you're doing? Count the number of eye rolls. If you receive less than three per day, then you're doing okay. And remember, you're trying to raise a money-smart, money-empowered kid, not to add unnecessary stress to your life.

Failure Happens

The idea that you must fail to succeed has become somewhat cliché. Seth Godin even describes a popular style of purposeful failure "performed" to generate attention—the currency of social media.[28] Yet real, meaningful failure remains a wise teacher. When you successfully give your kids control of their money, you court failure.

We should be okay with our kids' making little mistakes with real money now. When your child purchases an item in which she quickly loses interest, you can gently turn her attention to it. The scourge of *stuff* is difficult to overcome, and these little lessons give her some perspective. Making small errors now can help her avoid life-changing mistakes later. Better to slip up with a My Colorful Unicorn set than to get saddled with insurmountable college loan debt.

Of course, nothing guarantees that bigger blunders won't occur. But opening up this dialogue with your child—and combining it with real-world, real-money lessons—will empower her and give her confidence in handling her money as she grows into adulthood.

Grit and the Growth Mindset

Intertwined with failure are two key concepts: grit and the growth mindset. On a basic level, grit means showing perseverance and resilience.[29] Saving for a goal requires learning to delay gratification. Delayed gratification requires children to develop perseverance. Resilience, especially for young kids, is mandatory to stave off spending urges for *stuff* they want *right now*.

When our younger daughter decided to pony up the money for the replacement GoPro camera, she displayed resilience. She had to restart saving for her own goal. Grit girds children to deal with failure effectively and to realize that seemingly catastrophic occurrences lose their intensity and importance with time. Ultimately, we hope our children discover that *stuff* doesn't really matter much...if at all.

Carol Dweck coined the term "growth mindset" in her seminal book, *Mindset: The New Psychology of Success*. She notes that "[One] thing exceptional people seem to have is a special talent for converting life's setbacks into future successes."[30] Her theory that effort is the key to success is at the core of her book's principles.

Dweck contrasts the fixed and growth mindsets. Fixed mindsetters believe traits are hardwired: "I'm terrible at saving for goals." "Money burns a hole in my pocket." Growth mindsetters believe abilities can be improved with effort: "I'm having trouble saving for this goal. I'm going to try using visualization to help me improve at it." "I'm spending too much. I'm going to wait a week before I buy something I want." In using an example from this book, kids with growth mindsets can learn to become faster gazelles, able to outrun the proverbial lion.

This growth doesn't happen overnight. Dweck notes, "People with the growth mindset know that it takes time for potential to flower."[31] We want our kids to develop key skills to enable them to learn to use money as a tool. To make mistakes. To show resilience. To grow into money-empowered young adults.

Mini-Memo from the Chief Mammal:
Mindset: The New Psychology of Success

If you are able to read only one of the recommended works I cite throughout this book, then I'd suggest *Mindset: The New Psychology of Success*. If "Parenting 101" were offered in school, then this book would be the required reading. *Mindset* helped me adjust my own thinking and vastly improved how my wife and I talk to our kids. I was shocked at how fixed my mindset was, and I'm grateful that Dweck's book is helping us instill the importance of effort and resilience in our children. *Mindset* can help your family thrive.

Celebrating Achievement

"Every overnight success I've spoken to, took 10-20 years to get there. BUT ONLY if they celebrated small successes along the way."

—James Altucher

We want our children to be intrinsically motivated, driven by the satisfaction of money-smart achievement (e.g. saving for a goal). Even so, rewarding your child for these accomplishments from time to time can be a good idea. Employing *unexpected* rewards can help you avoid short circuiting her intrinsic motivation.

In his book *Drive: The Surprising Truth About What Motivates Us*, Dan Pink explains that unanticipated rewards, in place of expected ones, help ensure behavior remains intrinsically motivated while also allowing for opportunities to celebrate achievement. Pink notes that extrinsic motivation (e.g. driven by the reward rather than by satisfaction) can ironically be demotivating. For example, research shows that paying for performance (such as grades) isn't effective in the long term.[32] What happens when the reward goes away? You want your child to be motivated by a desire to learn, not by a desire to gobble up a reward of chicken nuggets.

We want to raise children who are motivated by learning or, similarly, by the satisfaction of reaching a goal. Consider helpful, unexpected "add-ons" as ways of celebrating achievement. If your son saves enough money for a new bike, then surprise him with a helmet. This practice is not only kind but also advisable.

One mom recalled a time when her daughter was agonizing over a purchase decision. She knew her daughter had only enough money to purchase one of the two items, yet her daughter didn't try to whine her into submission. Mom sympathized with her daughter's thoughtful consideration and appreciated her money-smart attitude. Mom felt compelled, in this one instance, to purchase the second item for her daughter. She felt this one-time reward wouldn't impede her daughter's progress toward money empowerment. Mom's action was such a rarity that the look on her daughter's face was priceless. Seeing that kind of appreciation is a wonderful thing to behold.

The Importance of Parental Attention

Research supports the importance of active parental involvement in a child's financial decisions. Merely providing an allowance does not change savings behavior. However, when a parent monitors his child's spending and educates his kid about the importance of saving, he is more likely to raise a money-smart child. In addition, kids who grow up in a money-smart environment have been shown to exhibit increased financial intelligence.[33] Who hasn't heard the cliché, "Kids do what we do and not what we say." We all have the scars to prove it!

All in the Families

Consider working with other parents in your neighborhood or with those of her school friends. Overcome the social taboos that make you feel like you shouldn't discuss money with other families. I've found most parents appreciate such conversations. They're concerned about the same issues as you.

You may face a problem when your daughter has a limited Breakthrough Allowance, and her friend has seemingly endless funds. This issue is especially difficult when you consider that most kids don't want unwarranted attention drawn to themselves, particularly money attention. Remember the story of the 48-year-old with money taboo issues who didn't want to come off as cheap? Taboos exist, and you're best off working to break them down. Make a plan. Coordinate. Share good ideas. Share mistakes. Rinse and repeat. When parents sync up their plans, allowance program sabotage becomes much more difficult, and teens' trips with their friends become *much* easier.

[28] "Seth Godin." *Design Matters with Debbie Millman*. *Design Observer*, February 6, 2017, http://www.debbiemillman.com/designmatters/seth-godin-2/.

[29] Duckworth, Angela L., Christopher Peterson, Michael D. Matthews, and Dennis R. Kelly. "Grit: Perseverance and Passion for Long-Term Goals." *Journal of Personality and Social Psychology* 92.6 (2007): 1087-1101.

[30] Dweck, Carol. *Mindset: The New Psychology of Success* (New York: Random House, 2006), 11.

[31] Dweck, *Mindset*, 28.

[32] Pink, *Drive*, 37-39.

[33] Drever et al., "Foundations," 21, 23, and 32.

Final Memo from the Chief Mammal:
Life Editing

*"Everything should be made as simple
as possible, but not simpler."*
—*Albert Einstein*

Graham Hill, founder of LifeEdited, describes how
to live a happier life by reducing reliance on *stuff* in
his hugely popular TED Talk. (See *theartofallowance.
com*.) Hill notes that we live in houses three
times bigger than they were in 1950, yet we
support a 22-trillion-dollar self-storage industry.[34]
To what end? Are we happier? More fulfilled? Are
we flourishing?

Elizabeth Dunn and Michael Norton, authors of
Happy Money: The Science of Happier Spending,
ingenuously organize their book around five big
money-related life hacks worth considering. These
tricks help us outsmart ourselves because, as Dan
Gilbert notes in *Stumbling on Happiness*, we're
surprisingly bad at knowing what will make us
happy in the future.[35]

We took the kids on a trip over the holidays. We
explained that the *experience* was the present. One
of Dunn and Norton's *Happy Money* hacks is to pay
for as much of the trip in advance to separate the
pain of paying from the euphoria of the trip. You
can also revel in anticipation—which is often as
good as, and sometimes better, than the trip itself.[36]

Our Christmas Day featured bike rides, board games and a home-cooked meal in a foreign country. But no presents! Of course, they're kids, so they certainly thought about what they had given up for the experience. However, they appreciated it and said they'd willingly make the trade-off again. Plus, we didn't drown in a sea of discarded wrapping paper.

To clarify, I am *not* anti-present. I have yet to run into a child who doesn't love getting gifts. The unnecessary *volume* of presents is a problem. Large amounts of gifts devalue each individual gift. We want to think through our purchases with a focus on quality over quantity. Evaluating each purchase we make is a sure sign of money-empowerment.

Mr. Money Mustache, a serious money maven with a silly name, has crafted a lifestyle business and blog aimed at changing the way we view work and retirement. He suggests we remove a negative when we make a purchase. For instance, building a detached home office may seem a bit extravagant when you consider his focus on an edited, sustainable life. Yet he explains that this action eliminated a major negative—a tight living situation that was causing severe family irritation. Conversely, the drone he considered buying, though fun, would not have removed any negatives.[37] The plaything also ran a high risk of becoming a forgotten bit of *stuff* in time.

Similarly, another *Happy Money* hack is to "buy time." Dunn and Norton reference poor time decisions, like driving an hour to get gas that is five cents cheaper per gallon or saving money on a flight that isn't non-stop when a slightly more expensive direct flight would save you time and frustration.[38]

Tim Ferriss of *Tools of Titans* and *The 4-Hour Workweek* fame suggests another hack—enjoy indulgences that are only marginally more expensive. For example, if you love chocolate, then purchasing *great* versus average chocolate is a matter of only a few dollars. Essentially, having "compartments of extravagance" is okay.[39]

"By consistently asking yourself how a purchase will affect your time, your dominant mind-set should shift, pushing you toward happier choices."[40] This statement, inspired by Dunn and Norton, is now one of my daily affirmations—a great example of *Spending Smart*. It's my everyday reminder to think smart about money.

Value is also important. When our daughter bought her scooter—one of her first goal achievements— she spent a little more money to get a Razor instead of a cheaper model that was popular due to aggressive marketing of the character featured on the handle. As you read earlier, she *still* rides that scooter because it was made well. (Also, there's no way she'd be riding a scooter with a smiling character from her early elementary days.) She remains pleased with having made a money-smart choice.

Interestingly, when I created the idea of a *Spend Smart* jar for our *Money Mammals* program, I was focused on helping kids make smarter, simpler money decisions. The good news is that *Spending Smart* has evolved into a family mantra. Although we're not always successful at avoiding *stuff*, we're more mindful of all our purchases.

[34] Hill, Graham. "Less Stuff. More Happiness." TED, March 2011, https://www.ted.com/talks/graham_hill_less_stuff_more_happiness.

[35] Gilbert, Dan. *Stumbling on Happiness*. New York: Random House, 2006.

[36] Dunn, Elizabeth and Michael Norton. *Happy Money: The Science of Happier Spending* (New York: Simon & Schuster, 2013), Chapter 4.

[37] "Mr. Money Mustache—Living Beautifully on $25-27K Per Year." *The Tim Ferriss Show with Tim Ferriss*. The Tim Ferriss Blog, February 13, 2017, http://tim.blog/2017/02/13/mr-money-mustache.

[38] Dunn and Norton, *Happy Money*, 54.

[39] "Mr. Money Mustache—Living Beautifully on $25-27K Per Year." *The Tim Ferriss Show with Tim Ferriss*. The Tim Ferriss Blog, February 13, 2017, http://tim.blog/2017/02/13/mr-money-mustache.

[40] Dunn and Norton, *Happy Money*, 76.

Thank You

I appreciate your taking the time to read this book. I hope it helps you help your child learn the core money-smart skills: *distinguishing needs from wants, making smart money choices* and *saving for goals*. I hope this book has given you a different perspective on money and the influence of *stuff* in our lives. Because you made it this far, I am confident you will be successful in raising a money-smart, money-empowered child.

I intend to refine and update this book as I learn more through continuing research on the subject and as I receive feedback from you and other readers. Please share your stories, both successes and failures, at *theartofallowance.com* as you make *The Art of Allowance* your own.

Yuval Harari, author of *Sapiens: A Brief History of Humankind*, calls money "the one story that everyone believes."[41] As long as that affirmation is true, money will be a part of all our own stories. My story. Your child's story. Your family's story.

We should never forget that money is a neutral player—neither good nor bad. Undoubtedly, a lack of money can be debilitating, so managing the money you have is important. But keep in mind that money doesn't make people smarter. Money doesn't make people better. Money, however, is a tool that your child must learn to use properly.

I hope you find this book to be a useful guide for helping you teach your child to use money as a tool. I hope you return to it again and again for tips, techniques and advice as you develop your unique *Art of Allowance*.

Most of all, I hope you are successful in raising a money-smart, money-empowered child.

Good luck.

Acknowledgements

I am so grateful for the input from many wonderful folks. Jackie Nagel, George Rand and Sylvia Jaunzarins helped me structure the book to identify key common threads, hopefully making it a more interesting and useful guide for you. Additional big thanks go out to Stephen King and Anne Lamott for their inspirational books (*On Writing: A Memoir of the Craft* and *Bird by Bird: Some Instructions on Writing and Life* respectively) about how they practice their craft.

Thanks also go to my dad, John Lanza, an author in his own right, for his edits as well as to my mom, Carolyn Thomas, my lifelong grammar checker. David McCurrach, Emily Smith, Erin Prim, Cecily Harrison and Sue Thorpe provided additional invaluable notes, ideas, edits and stories. Thank you!

The biggest thanks must go to my wife, Eileen, and our two daughters, Quinn and Kellyn. Eileen is right up there with my grandfather in terms of money smarts, and I can only hope that we are raising our kids to follow in her (and perhaps our) footsteps. I am so fortunate to have you all in my life.

Todd Slater, a good friend and talented artist, made this book look great. I have to thank him and the rest of our *Money Mammals* team for all the hard work in making our program a reality.

You can find the resources discussed in this book, my blog and more at *theartofallowance.com*.

About the Author

John Lanza is the Chief Mammal of Snigglezoo Entertainment and author and co-illustrator of the acclaimed "Share & Save & Spend Smart" *Money Mammals* children's picture book series, featuring the Dr. Toy award-winning *Joe the Monkey Saves for a Goal, Joe the Monkey Learns to Share* and *Joe the Monkey and Friends Learn About Spending Smart.*

John created *The Money Mammals "Saving Money Is Fun"* DVD and founded *The Money Mammals* Saving Money Is Fun Kids Club, which is partnered with credit unions nationwide. John is a recognized thought leader in youth financial literacy. He and his *Money Mammals* have been featured by *The New York Times, The Wall Street Journal* and *The Los Angeles Times,* among others.

Suggested Reading

Happy Money: The Science of Happier Spending, Elizabeth Dunn & Michael Norton

Mindset: The New Psychology of Success, Carol Dweck

Stumbling on Happiness, Daniel Gilbert

Sapiens: A Brief History of Humankind, Yuval Harari

"Motivation Theory Applied to the Allowance/Chore Debate," Karyn Hodgens

The Life-Changing Magic of Tidying Up: The Japanese Art of Decluttering and Organizing, Marie Kondo

The Opposite of Spoiled: Raising Kids Who Are Grounded, Generous, and Smart About Money, Ron Lieber

Allowance Magic: Turn Your Kids into Money Wizards, David McCurrach

The First National Bank of Dad, David Owen

Drive: The Surprising Truth About What Motivates Us, Daniel Pink

Nudge: Improving Decisions About Health, Wealth, and Happiness, Richard Thaler & Cass Sunstein

Money Mammals Products

The Money Mammals "Saving Money Is Fun" (Children's DVD)

Joe the Monkey Saves for a Goal (Children's Book)

Joe the Monkey Learns to Share (Children's Book)

Joe the Monkey and Friends Learn About Spending Smart (Children's Book)

The Money Mammals For Your FAMILY! Kit (Family Resource)

The Money Mammals Teaching Kit (Educational Resource)

Save for a Goal (Downloadable App)

Currency Challenge (Downloadable App)

Needs vs. Wants (Downloadable App)

Vargas' Money Drop (Downloadable App)

My Disclaimer

I have read and heard many ideas since beginning this journey to help families raise money-smart, money-empowered kids. I have cited the original thoughts and ideas of others to the best of my ability. There are many concepts that are now standards of youth financial literacy. These guidelines are not cited in the book. Please let me know if I have forgotten to cite or have incorrectly cited someone or something, and I'll do my best to correct any transgressions in future editions. No omission was intentional.

My intention was to write a book that provides a practical framework for giving your child an allowance to put her on a path to becoming a money-smart, money-empowered child while also addressing larger themes like the role of money in society and the proliferation of *stuff* in our lives. For that reason, this book may cause you to reevaluate your own financial plans. Please consult with a financial or investment professional before engaging in any decisions that might affect your own financial well-being.

John

---

41 "Reality and the Imagination: A Conversation with Yuval Noah Harari." *Waking Up with Sam Harris.* Sam Harris, March 19, 2017, https://www.samharris.org/podcast/item/reality-and-the-imagination.

www.ingramcontent.com/pod-product-compliance
Lightning Source LLC
Chambersburg PA
CBHW071232090426
42736CB00014B/3050